DALE JENKINS

IMMERSE

A SIMPLE LOOK AT BAPTISM

ISBN-13: 9781071459799

Published by The Jenkins Institute

thejenkinsinstitute.com

Cover Design: Andrew Jenkins
Interior Layout: Joey Sparks

Special Thanks:
Bob Pritchard, Shannon O'Bryan,
Kaitlyn Rose Richardson, Ben Thompson, and
Jon Mitchell for their help with editing and
questions

DEDICATION

We halfway jokingly nicknamed him "aqua-man." John Kerr practiced medicine in the little town of Hamilton, Alabama for his whole career, 40 years. He is a good doctor but a better lover of souls. He just wants people to go to heaven. He talked to all of his patients about Jesus. He wasn't harsh or judgmental, he just wants people to go to heaven. But that isn't where he got the nickname. It came on a trip to Russia in 1995. He led more people to Christ than the rest of the group put together. He excelled on the mission field. He loved the hunger that people in other countries seemed to have for the Word of God. I remember the day we sat in his car and he wept as talked about how he wished he could go to more mission points but how he could make enough in one week at his clinic to support multiple missionaries. He followed what he could do versus what he wanted to do.

I joyfully dedicate this book to Dr. John M. Kerr, a friend of every good work and a lover of souls.

WITH THANKS

A book is never the product of one person. This book is no different. I want to thank Joey Sparks who handles details I cannot. My son Andrew designed the cover of this one. And the supporters of TheJenkinsInstitute.com are always essential to providing the gifts that make it possible for us to provide materials to churches and individuals so affordably. Finally, I thank my mom and dad. I have a friend who always includes in his prayers those who cared enough about him to teach him the Gospel. I concur. I wish everyone could grow up in a truly Christian home.

CONTENTS

INTRODUCTION

Thanks for picking up this book. We may have never even met, but I know something about you. You are interested in your soul. I can't imagine any other reason someone would pick up this book (well, unless your kin to me, and if that's it, hey).

If we were sitting across from each other there are plenty of things we could talk about but not a one as important as the subject of our souls. And if we were sitting across from each other, I would have a big smile on my face and, I would love you. I want to go over a couple of things with you up front.

We can get a lot of things wrong in life and be OK, but there is no subject more important than our salvation. But even then, I want you to know that I will not judge you, that's God's arena and not ours (Matthew 7:1; Hebrews 9:27).

While I want to talk to you straight I also have no desire to be mean or offensive. I don't have any desire to win an argument, I would never purposely hurt you or offend you. But to quote a preacher from a long time ago: "I would rather have thousands to say to me at the judgment, 'We heard you preach, and you hurt our feelings,' than to have just one soul to say, 'I heard you preach, but you did not tell me the truth'" (John T. Lewis).

I also want you to know that I don't have anything to gain with this book. I don't get a raise based on how many people I lead to Christ, and I'm not making money off books. So, the only agenda I have in writing is for us to try to understand this Bible subject better.

We are going to talk about baptism. Some of you may think we talk about it too much, and I imagine for many of you reading this it is mentioned in every worship service you attend. But there is a difference between mentioning something and talking about it. I hope to be able to answer many of your questions and that if you have any when we are done you'll talk with someone more about this. If you want to talk with me, my cell phone number is 615 294-1453 and you can text me or call me.

I want to ask something I've never asked before in book form; will you take a moment a pray about this study?

LESSON 1

WHO'S IN CHARGE AROUND HERE?

WHERE DO WE START?

My dad led more people to Jesus than anyone I know. I loved learning from Him how to share the story of Jesus and help people come to faith. He would talk about living a life consistent with what you teach. He loved to talk to people from an attitude of "we are learning about Jesus together." But I want to share with you what he said was the single most significant thing in bringing people to Jesus. OK? Before you can have a study with someone you have to establish Bible authority.

In dad's book he wrote to help people understand God's way to Him he started this way: "The God who took the time to create man and send His son to redeem man would surely, if He had the power and desire, communicate with man. The Scriptures reveal that God has both the ability and desire to communicate with man. The Scriptures teach that indeed God does speak to us. Since God does speak today what method does He use?"

Remember Snopes? It's still around but for the longest time, it was the "go-to place" when you needed to check out a rumor or a story that was going around. Was Disney giving away free admissions tickets if you had 1,000 retweets? Was Facebook going to start charging? Check out Snopes. Was there a little boy with cancer who wanted to set a record for the number of cards received? Look at Snopes. Then it happened. It was found out that Snopes was actually a couple who would google info to find stuff or at best a company with highly-biased "fact-checkers." It sort of lost its mystique and credibility.[1] The source we thought was an authority wasn't at all. It didn't stand the test of time and reliability.

IT'S A BAD WORD, A VERY BAD WORD?

While authority can be misused and is a negative word to some people, it is, in fact, a really important word. It is a word that determines things: Things like, how tall you are, who caught the biggest fish, who had the fastest time in the race, what you will be paid for the work you do, and what size clothes you need to buy online. Without an authority, you have no standard.

For just about any discussion you have to determine who or what the final word is. What is the standard or authority?

You may not like rules but imagine..
   ...driving without them. If a green light means "go" to you but a red light means "go" to the person you meet at an intersection, without an authority, how would you know who had the right of way? It would be a nightmare at every intersection.

...trying to play a sport without them. What if you were competing in the long jump but there was no standard to determine how long a meter or a foot was.

...trying to bake a cake without them. A pound of sugar might be called for in a recipe, but what if the person who wrote the recipe thought a pound was 72 oz and you thought it was 7 oz?

...OR worse than any of these, imagine trying to please God when He has not said what He expects. Just guessing could be really dangerous.

Authority determines rules, and while sometimes it may seem to you that rules get in the way, the truth is they actually keep us from constant arguments and unresolvable disagreements. Correct authority solves so many problems.

We want and need a trusted and worthy authority. I think you'd agree this is especially true spiritually.

The great news of today's class is that God has spoken. He has told us what He expects of us and where to find that. Hebrews 1 says that God has spoken. But the question is: How has He spoken? Or, How does God speak today?

Hebrews 1:1-2 says *"Long ago, at many times and in many ways, God spoke to our fathers by the prophets, but in these last days he has spoken to us by his Son, whom he appointed the heir of all things, through whom also he created the world."* So, to be clear, TODAY, God speaks through His Son, Jesus.

But how does Jesus speak to us?
Jesus speaks today through His apostles, the ones He selected and gave the mission of bringing His message. Jesus knew that the apostles would not remember everything they had learned from Him, so He sent them the Holy Spirit (John 14:26). And the Holy Spirit guided these men into ALL TRUTH. In John 16:13 Jesus told the

apostles: *"When the Spirit of truth comes, he will guide you into all the truth, for he will not speak on his own authority, but whatever he hears he will speak, and he will declare to you the things that are to come."*

And these men wrote down what the Spirit told them to. Read Ephesians 3:1-6.

Today these writings, the Scriptures or the Bible furnish us with what we need: *"All Scripture is breathed out by God and profitable for teaching, for reproof, for correction, and for training in righteousness, that the man of God may be complete, equipped for every good work"* (2 Timothy 3:16-17).

So, each of the New Testament writers was inspired (note: Inspired = God-breathed).

In fact, Peter (another apostle) told us that God has *"given us all things that pertain to life and godliness"* (2 Peter 1:3).

And, on top of that, we will be judged by the things written in the Bible: *"And I saw the dead, great and small, standing before the throne, and books were opened. Then another book was opened, which is the book of life. And the dead were judged by what was written in the books, according to what they had done"* (Revelation 20:12; also read John 12:48).

You could say it looks a little like this:

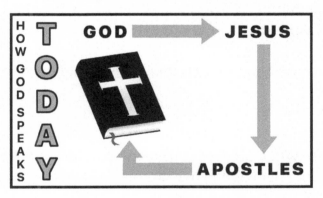

What does all this have to do with the title on the cover?

There are a lot of people who say a lot of

things about baptism. Some of those people are really smart, some are really good communicators, some are even religious leaders, BUT if they say something different than the Bible, we have to remember that they are not the final word, the authority.

If we are going to have any kind of good class this week we have to agree on an authority For this week, the final word on a matter where God has spoken will be His Word.

So on baptism–what does the Bible say?

THINK IT OUT:
1. What kind of authority do we have to establish when we are trying to talk to someone about God?

2. What does authority mean?

3. How does God speak to us today?

4. What will we be judged by? See John 12:48

5. What would your life look like if there were no rules? If you didn't have an authority?

A LITTLE DEEPER

1. What are some ways people say God speaks today that the Bible does not say?

2. What if my preacher or parent says something different from what the Bible teaches?

3. Jesus said the Spirit would guide the apostles into all truth (John 16:13). What is truth? See John 17:17

4. Proverbs 14:12 says, "There is a way that seems right to a man, but its end is the way of death." Why is it that what seems right to us oftentimes is not the way to go?

5. Proverbs 3:5-6 says we should *"trust in God with all our heart rather than leaning on*

our own understanding, and that we should acknowledge Him in all our ways." How does one acknowledge God in every decision they make rather than leaning on their own understanding?

[1]*https://www.forbes.com/sites/kalevleetaru/2016/12/22/the-daily-mail-snopes-story-and-fact-checking-the-fact-checkers/#10368833227f*

LESSON 2

WHAT IS BIBLE BAPTISM?

WHAT'S IT ALL ABOUT?

It is NOT our goal to see how many people we can baptize. If that was the goal then we'd just offer a nice new crisp $100 bill to anyone who was baptized and the number would sky-rocket. In fact, some of you would be baptized 5 or 10 times, right?

It is our goal to get people to believe in Jesus. See, that is ultimately what baptism is all about. Jesus' best friend when He was on earth explained why he wrote a book about Jesus: *"...these are written so that you may believe that Jesus is the Christ, the Son of God, and that by believing you may have life in his name"* (John 20:31; please also read John 1:12). Another of the apostles, Peter said *"... there is salvation in no one else, for there is no other name under heaven given among men by which we must be saved"* (Acts 4:12).

It is about Faith! Don't let anyone kid you or mislead you. It is all about Faith! We'll get to baptism, but how we get there is by believing in Jesus completely. See, when we say "believing in Jesus" we are saying much more than just saying that He existed (every legitimate historian knows that. Even the devil knows that, James 2:19).

Let me jump ahead now and just say we are talking about a kind of belief, a faith, so convinced that Jesus is God's Son, that He was killed and came back to life (was resurrected), that you will do whatever He says. Actually, the natural and commanded action of real belief is baptism. Acts 8 talks about a man who went to a place where Jesus had never been preached about and, well, just listen: *"...when they believed Philip as he preached good news about the kingdom of God and the name of Jesus Christ, they were*

baptized, both men and women" (Acts 8:12).
Paul, yet another inspired apostle, wrote: *"I am not ashamed of the gospel, for it is the power of God for salvation to everyone who believes, to the Jew first and also to the Greek. For in it the righteousness of God is revealed from faith for faith, as it is written, 'The righteous shall live by faith'"* (Romans 1:16–17, emp. dj). Notice a few things about that verse. One: The word gospel, that word means good news, whether you are a Christian now or become one later, never forget that. This is not bad news, it is good news that we believe in. Two: Notice, that Greek in that verse means anyone not a Jew. That means everyone who reads this book will fall into one category or the other.

There are many other verses about faith we could look at, but one more before we move forward: *"...without faith it is impossible to please him, for whoever would draw near to God must believe that he exists and that he rewards those who seek him"* (Hebrews 11:6).

"YOU GET A CAR, AND YOU GET A CAR, AND YOU GET A CAR!"

Faith is sort of like that famous Oprah show where everybody got a car. Everybody has faith. You have faith and the person sitting beside you has faith, and your girlfriend or boyfriend has faith, the President has faith and so did Aldoph Hitler and Osama bin Laden.

Everyone has faith. We live by faith! When you stumbled or bolted out of bed this morning and your feet hit the floor you had faith that the earth would support your weight. When you ate breakfast, it may not have tasted as good as you wished, but you ate it never thinking it would poison you. You had faith.

Everyone has faith. The question is, what do you have faith in and is it worthy of and strong enough for you to put your faith there? Is it trustworthy? Can it support you?

Your decision to accept the Bible: that's a matter of faith! Ultimately faith is a belief that leads to an action. Say that again. Faith is a belief that leads to an action. James was talking about faith and said it this way: *"But someone will say, 'You have faith and I have works.' Show me your faith apart from your works, and I will show you my faith by my works...Do you want to be shown, you foolish person, that faith apart from works is useless?"* (James 2:18 & 20). See, what James is saying is that you can tell me all day long you believe in Jesus, but unless you do what He says, you really don't. Faith is actionable! As a side note, for those who argue that baptism is a work and that salvation is not to be works based, notice that James indicates that faith itself is a work. Notice, it is not the work of faith that saves a person, it is God, through Christ, but without faith you can't be saved.

So what is the working faith that saves?

Quickly here is what Jesus said you have to do: He said you have to repent (Luke 13:3). To repent really just means to change your mind and your actions follow. Imagine we're in a car and everyone says they want to go to McD's, but on the way, we see Taco Bell and everyone changed their mind about McD's. We've "repented" of McD's and our actions back that up as now we're headed to Taco Bell. In pleasing God that simply means you make a decision to try to stop doing anything wrong you were doing and you try to live right because it's wrong living (sin) that hurts Jesus (Hebrews 6:6).

Jesus also said you have to be willing to confess that you believe He is God's Son (Matthew 10:32). Again, that means you are willing to own that you believe in Him in front of other people. So, when all the guys are telling dirty jokes or the girls are gossiping and cutting on someone, you own up to the fact that Jesus is God's Son and act like you believe that. Confession is a statement but it is also followed by an action. Or we might say it this way, we make our confession and then we live out our confession.

Jesus also said you have to be baptized (Matthew 28:18-20; Mark 16:16). For some reason, many people don't have any issue with doing any of the other things I just mentioned but this one trips them up. In fact, many of your friends in other churches think you "have to" believe and repent and confess but don't think baptism is a "have to" thing. Even though Jesus, Himself, said *"he who believes in me and is baptized will be saved"* (Mark 16:16).

Baptism, that's such an odd word.

You're right. In fact, did you know you can speak Greek? Say it: baptism. See, you can. It's actually not really an English word.

When the most popular translation of the Bible from Greek to English was produced, the guys who did it were all a part of a church that did not baptize at all. And they were afraid if they translated that word of what would happen so they just took the Greek word (baptizo, the original Greek word) and wrote it in English letters and came up with the word baptize. It'd be like saying agua instead of saying water all the time. You'd be right, but it'd be a little odd if you only spoke English to always use a Spanish word.

BIBLE BAPTISM:

So, what did Baptizo (that original Greek word) mean? It meant to immerse. Plan and simple. There is no question about it. And the word is used almost 100 times in the Bible and every time it simply means to immerse (so, without getting too far ahead, if you were sprinkled or christened instead of being immersed, you were not baptized by the very meaning of the word. I'm not trying to start a fight with anyone, just stating the fact. That is between you and God and you and your parents).

Remember, the Bible is our authority in this study, so let me tell you five things about baptism that the Bible tells us.

1. Bible baptism is by the authority of Jesus (Matthew 28:18-20).

2. Bible baptism is only for those who believe Jesus is God's Son at the time of their baptism (Mark 16:16; Acts 8:37).

This means that if a person is a baby and is baptized it is not Bible baptism. It may be special and it may be sweet and it may be meaningful to those who see it and that baby may someday believe in Jesus, but that act was not Bible baptism).

3. Bible baptism is in water (Acts 8:38-39).

4. Bible baptism is immersion. If the word study above wasn't enough just read Romans 6:3-4 that states it real clear. *"Do you not know that all of us who have been baptized into Christ Jesus were baptized into his death? We were buried therefore with him by baptism into death, in order that, just as Christ was raised from the dead by the glory of the Father, we too might walk in newness of life"* (Romans 6:3-4).

Apart from what this verse proves about the "action" of baptism, it is just a beautiful picture of how baptism helps us identify with Jesus.

5. Bible baptism is for the forgiveness of sins (Acts 2:38). So, while we may get a lot of folks to be baptized by passing out $100's it wouldn't be Bible baptism. And while your friend being baptized might make you start thinking about being baptized, if the only reason you are baptized is that your friend was or you think it would make others around you happy, that would not be Bible baptism.

At this point I have to say the most challenging thing for many that I will say in this book. There are many large and powerful religious groups who baptize BECAUSE a person has been saved. They believe and teach that a person is saved and then at some point they ought to be baptized.

But that is not what Peter taught in Acts 2 on the birthday of the church. It is not what Jesus told His disciples to model when He gave them their marching orders. Therefore, if you were told you were saved and then that at some point later you should be baptized and you were, it was not Bible baptism.

I am not questioning your sincerity nor that of the person who told that to you, I'm just saying we agreed that in this study the Bible would be our authority and in the Bible baptism was always FOR the forgiveness of sins and not BECAUSE of the forgiveness of sins.

May I go one step further? If you question this, go to the person who baptized you and ask them. They will tell you plainly what they did or believed they were doing when they baptized you. And if it is not what the Bible says then why would you not take care of this matter?

This is the most important decision in your life! There are many reasons to become a Christian, like the fear of being lost (Mark 16:16), the rewards of the abundant Christian life, or the joy of being with other Christians, but the greatest of all reasons for becoming a Christian is a loving appreciation for what Jesus did at Calvary. He died on the cross for you and to make it possible for you to have your sins forgiven and to go to heaven.

READY WHEN YOU ARE!

If you want to be baptized and all of that makes sense to you, there is NOTHING we are doing as a minister, church leader, teacher, church, or Christian friend that is more important than talking to you about that! So, ask. We will be happy about that! If you have questions ask, that is why we are here.

One more thing here. Jesus said, *"if you love me, keep my commandments"* (John 14:15). Is there any reason why you should not be baptized like the Bible teaches?

I've talked to hundreds of thousands of people and have never talked to any one who has regretted becoming a Christian. But I have talked to people who regretted waiting to become one.

THINK ABOUT IT:
1. What is baptism ultimately about?

2. What is the natural response (or action) to real faith?

3. What does "gospel" mean?

4. What 3 things does Jesus say to do if you believe?

5. What are a few things that Bible baptism is according to this chapter?

6. How does obeying what Jesus says to do prove that you really believe in Him?

7. How does the concept of repentance go along with how Paul describes us being baptized "into death" (Romans 6:3-7)?

8. How does the literal definition of baptism (immersion) go along with how Paul describes baptism as a burial in Romans 6:4?

9. How is obeying Jesus' command to be baptized a sign that your faith in Him is not dead (James 2:14-26)?

10. Why do you think some people have a problem with the idea that one has to be baptized in order to be saved, even though Jesus said that?

LESSON 3

VERSES ABOUT BAPTISM:
WHAT DOES THE BIBLE SAY?

If you've been paying attention you have learned that we practice baptism by immersion. We celebrate baptisms. In fact, in every sermon you hear preached here you'll hear us talk about baptism.

I want to explain in very clear and simple terms why it is that preachers of the Gospel put so much emphasis on baptism. We're going to talk about what Jesus taught about baptism. After all, He is our example.

Can we agree that if Jesus said it was important, it is important? Regardless of what anyone else or any church might say or do? So if I can't show you from the life of Jesus that baptism is important then maybe we shouldn't make such a big fuss about it and just do it instead.

But first, let me mention a common view about baptism. Some say "Baptism is important but it's not necessary." The people who hold that view would never say that belief is not necessary, or repentance is important but not necessary. They would never say, I think a person ought to believe in Jesus, but they can be OK without it. But they will argue that baptism is important, but that it's not necessary. Even though in the New Testament there is no such thing as an unbaptized Christian. They would say it is not essential.

I do not question the sincerity of those who believe this but remember we are looking for Bible answers, not our opinions. Whenever we're confused about anything we ought to always go first to Jesus. He is our example and He is the author & finisher of our Faith (Hebrews 12:1).

We'll start in Matthew 3 with the baptism of Jesus himself (read Matthew 3:13-17). In verse 11 John had just said that Jesus was going to come as a baptizer, so John's first reaction was, "you shouldn't be baptized by me, I should be baptized by you." Why would Jesus submit to baptism, especially when John was baptizing for the forgiveness of sins and Jesus had committed no sins?

There are a plenty of ideas and theories as to why Jesus was baptized, but here's the bottom line, Jesus explains it Himself: "Let's do this to fulfill all righteousness." One translation says "Please do it, for I must do all that is right."

In other words, Jesus said, it is right for me to seek you out and be baptized. and the text makes it clear, God was pleased that Jesus did this and it fulfilled the Father's Will. So, behind every baptism of a believer is the baptism of Jesus. Jesus came to John and said: "You must baptize me for this is right."

That's at the start of Matthew's account of the Gospel but if you will look at the end of his book. Matthew 28:18-20, these are the last words of Jesus that Matthew records. It seems significant that at the beginning of Matthew's gospel and at the end of Matthew's gospel we have an emphasis on baptism. Jesus said, *"I want you to make disciples, baptizing them into the name of the Father and the Son and the Holy Spirit."*

"Into the name" was a business term, it meant "to move ownership." Baptism is where believers make a public statement that my life is now under new ownership, my life is now being managed, by Christ.

Jesus made baptism an indispensable part of the making disciples process. It is always necessary to imitate Jesus and obey what He says.

Now read Mark 16:15-16. Baptism is not the good news (Gospel = good news). The good news is of the gospel is the story of the death and resurrection of Jesus (see 1 Corinthians 15:1-4). The good news is that in His sinless Son, God has made a way for your sin debt to be paid so that you can be saved and so that you can avoid punishment.

But NOTICE, Jesus expects that when people hear the good news they are going to respond by believing and being baptized. Notice, in the Bible anytime baptism is mentioned there is a close connection between it and faith. The construction here in Mark 16 won't allow you to make either one either more important or less important than the other. You must put the same emphasis on baptism that you do on believing. The person is either going to do both or he's not going to do either.

Baptism is God promising to do something

for us when we show faith in the gospel. In the book of John, a man named Nicodemus comes to talk to Jesus and Jesus said *"Truly, truly, I say to you, unless one is born again he cannot see the kingdom of God...unless one is born of water and the Spirit, he cannot enter the kingdom of God"* (John 3:3-5). Jesus called this new birth a birth of water and of the Spirit. Now notice, baptism is not a work added to faith it is a result of or a part of the expression of your faith.

Baptism is a faith response to the gospel. I think it's interesting that in this same chapter, John 3, we find what may be the most famous words of the Bible, *"For God so loved the world that whoever believes in Him will not perish but have eternal life"* (v. 16).

Let me show you a Bible example. Turn to Acts 16 and read verses 29-34. The jailer asked the men, "What must I do to be saved?" Paul and Silas said that you must believe – but what does he do immediately? He is baptized. And he's filled with joy because it says, he believes.

Baptism pictures powerfully the death, burial, and resurrection of Jesus. Paul says it in Romans 6:3–4. Every time someone is baptized it reenacts the gospel! That's why we practice baptism, it is our way of saying "the gospel is true!" We are mirroring the very actions of Jesus saving us.

One more thing: baptism says salvation is free because Jesus is our Savior. Ephesians 2:8–9 says: *"For by grace you have been saved through faith. And this is not your own doing; it is the gift of God, not a result of works, so that no one may boast."*

Baptism doesn't contradict that verse, it endorses it. Have you ever considered how passive a person is at baptism? It's not something you do, it's something done to you. In baptism, Jesus has acted and you are the recipient. It is a gift. It's as if Jesus is saying "you just relax and I'll do the rest. TRUST ME." Baptism is God saying, you just follow and I'll do the rest. No one takes a victory lap in the baptistry showing off what a great thing THEY have done. The command is to be baptized and show we believe the gospel.

All of this may have raised some questions like: If Jesus emphasized baptism so much, why don't more churches emphasize it? Almost all churches say baptism is important but few talk about it very much or teach it is essential. Why is that? I think one reason is a fear of promoting works righteousness. We don't want to imply that we are saved by what we do but by what Jesus did. And since so many people misunderstand baptism to be a work rather than an act of faith, they are afraid that emphasizing baptism will take the focus off the cross. Now, we don't want to do that. We don't want baptism to make the cross seem unimportant. We contend that baptism affirms the cross. That baptism is my act of faith or truth in what Jesus did for me at the cross.

Now, we don't want to say more about baptism than the Bible does, but neither would any of us want to water down what the Bible really does say about baptism. So now we are going to walk through some of the significant texts of the New Testament about baptism. We won't have time to look at all of them but I think you will see again that there is a reason why we need to preach what we practice.

Since the Bible is our authority in this class, let's look at what several Bible verses say about baptism. Let's start in Acts 2, what we call the birthday of the church. This is obviously a significant time. Peter preaches the first Gospel sermon and the listeners are convicted and say "what should we do?" Peter replied in Acts 2:38

"repent and be baptized." Some people struggle with the idea that baptism has anything to do with salvation. So, they will say that Peter didn't really mean "repent and be baptized for the remission of sins" but "repent and be baptized because your sins are forgiven." The only problem with that is it goes completely against the text. The text doesn't imply that in any way - in fact, it says just the opposite.

Or next text is found in 1 Corinthians 1:13-15. Some would say, "Well that verse says baptism isn't very important after all, Paul said he was glad he didn't baptize many." The fact that he doesn't remember who he baptized actually helps our study of its importance. Everyone was baptized, so Paul didn't remember which of them he had baptized.

The next verse is Galatians 3:26-27. Notice it does not say all who have been clothed with Christ are then baptized but that all who have been baptized have been clothed with Christ. The idea is that baptism joins us, clothes us, unities us, identifies us with Christ.

The next text would be Ephesians 4:4-6. Here, Paul mentions seven ones. Notice the high company with which baptism is placed. It's interesting that there are those who debate about baptism would not dare to debate the place or importance of any of the other six words. "Well, there is One God but you know He is not essential." Or, "Of course it says there is One Faith but I certainly wouldn't want to overemphasize the necessity of the role of faith!" NO, nobody would say that.

That's why I hope if you have not been baptized you will think about this and maybe even make your commitment known today. The Christian life is GREAT! You will never regret the decision to become a Child of our King!

NOTE: The construction of this chapter is due to a sermon I heard on tape several years back. I do not know the source of that tape.

THINK ABOUT IT:

1. Why was Jesus baptized?

2. What does Jesus say at the end of Matthew?

3. What does "into the name" mean?

4. What does Peter tell those who ask what they must do to be saved?

5. Psalm 119:172 says that all of God's commandments are right. If Jesus was baptized "in order to fulfill all righteousness," wouldn't that mean that baptism would be something God commanded and thus is right?

6. Read 1 Corinthians 1:10–17. Do you think that the division and undue loyalty to the people who had taught and baptized them the reason Paul was thankful he had not baptized many of the Corinthians?

7. Ephesians 4:5 says there is "one baptism." How many baptisms are therefore valid in the sight of God? Who defines what the "one baptism" is? Where

is the only place you find the information about the "one baptism"?

8. Jesus died on the cross, was buried in a tomb, and was raised to a new life 3 days later. How does baptism reenact that (Romans 6:3-5)?

9. When the Jews asked Peter, "What shall we do?" (Acts 2:37), did Peter tell them to just believe in Jesus? Did he tell them to pray a prayer in order for their sins to be forgiven? What did he tell them to do? Why?

LESSON 4

YOU'VE GOT QUESTIONS?

What is baptism?

You know, I've been studying the Bible pretty much all of my life. I know how it is. We forget things. And, it seems now-a-days we rarely really slow down. So you might have missed what we've seen so far.

So, a 45-second review: Bible baptism: Is always immersion, in water, by the authority of Jesus Christ, of a believer, for the forgiveness of sins of one who has determined to live for Jesus. There are about 100 verses in the Bible on it. And while he would NEVER diminish the importance of confession (he was the model of that, Matthew 16:16-18). Peter summed it up this way *"Baptism, which corresponds to this, now saves you, not as a removal of dirt from the body but as an appeal to God for a good conscience, through the resurrection of Jesus Christ"* (1 Peter 3:21).

Yet there are still people who question the significance of baptism:

Have you ever thought, "I just wish we could really know what the truth is about baptism?" Obviously, these are mock interviews designed to help make the point, but imagine if we could have a conversation with a few of the people who were there when Jesus taught.

If we're going big, the first one we'd want to talk to is THE ONE, Jesus Himself.

YOU: "Jesus, if baptism is really important why didn't you make it simpler to understand that it is essential?"
JESUS: *"He who believes and is baptized shall be saved."* I'm not sure I could have made

that any clearer.

YOU: "Peter, you were the first to preach about Jesus as the way of salvation after the resurrection. I just wish, on that first day, you would have told in a clear way what someone who believes Jesus is God's Son was supposed to do."

PETER: *"'Let all the house of Israel therefore know for certain that God has made him both Lord and Christ, this Jesus whom you crucified.' Now when they heard this they were cut to the heart, and said to Peter and the rest of the apostles, 'Brothers, what shall we do?' And Peter said to them, 'Repent and be baptized every one of you in the name of Jesus Christ for the forgiveness of your sins, and you will receive the gift of the Holy Spirit'"* (Acts 2:36–38).

YOU: "Peter, help me to understand. I mean it sounded like you were saying baptism is a command. I just wish you had commanded it."

PETER: I *"declared, 'Can anyone withhold*

water for baptizing these people, who have received the Holy Spirit just as we have?' And he commanded them to be baptized in the name of Jesus Christ" (Acts 10:46–48).

YOU: "Sorry to bother you again about this but do you really believe baptism is the action that finally saves a person?"

PETER: *"Baptism, which corresponds to this, now saves you, not as a removal of dirt from the body but as an appeal to God for a good conscience, through the resurrection of Jesus Christ"* (1 Peter 3:21).

YOU: "Paul, people say you are the most influential person outside of Christ on Christianity. If anybody had this figured out, a brainiac[1] like you would have. Does baptism really affect our relationship with Jesus?"

PAUL: *"For as many of you as were baptized into Christ have put on Christ"* (Galatians 3:27).

YOU: "You really lived for Jesus. You loved to tell the story of Jesus and His impact on your life. It's really beautiful how you went from persecuting Christians to living for Christ full-throttle. It would have been great if in telling that story you could have said something about whether baptism was important."

PAUL: God told me to wait for instructions and he sent *"Ananias, a devout man ... And he said, 'The God of our fathers appointed you to know his will, to see the Righteous One and to hear a voice from his mouth; for you will be a witness for him to everyone of what you have seen and heard. And now why do you wait? Rise and be baptized and wash away your sins, calling on his name'"* (Acts 22:12, 14-16).

YOU: "OK, Paul, I'm beginning to see what you are saying. One more question: It seems like maybe some mystical encounter might be more experiential. Does baptism really help us identify with Jesus?"

PAUL: *"Do you not know that all of us who have*

been baptized into Christ Jesus were baptized into his death? We were buried therefore with him by baptism into death, in order that, just as Christ was raised from the dead by the glory of the Father, we too might walk in newness of life. For if we have been united with him in a death like his, we shall certainly be united with him in a resurrection like his" (Romans 6:3-5).

I'm really not trying to argue or be snarky, or cute here but how could God have made it clearer that it is absolutely essential that you be immersed?[2] The question isn't do you need to know more, but what are you doing with what you already know?

BUT what about...?

There are always some honest questions. We'll try to answer them a few here. Remember, we're not trying to argue or explain something away but to honestly let the text be our guide, our authority.

What about the thief on the cross? Somebody told me he wasn't baptized but he was saved.

I think that's a great question. Dr. Luke records the event in Luke 22:32, 39-43. A few things stand out. One, Jesus can save anyone He wants to (see Luke 5:23-24). Two, the thief on the cross lived under the Old Law and baptism was not a part of that law. Read Hebrews 9:15-17 and notice that Jesus had not yet died and brought in the new covenant. So, he, unlike us, was not commanded to be baptized.

What about someone who dies on the way to the baptistry?

First off, this is not really a good question.

It is designed to add emotion to a question to make you think the answer would be different because of the emotion. I've heard the question for nearly 50 years but NEVER heard of it happening a single time.

But, and let us be clear here when we talk about baptism and it being absolutely essential, we are not judging another. That is not our job. I sort of like what Barak Obama said once when asked a certain question: "That's above my pay grade." My job, our job and mission is to teach what we understand the Bible to teach. It is up to others to obey and up to God to decide who is lost and saved.

What about the people in Acts 10? They received the Holy Spirit so it is clear they were saved before they were baptized. Would that not be evidence that one is saved before baptism?

No. In fact, Peter commanded that they be baptized. If baptism was not absolutely essential he would not have done that with this group. Just read the text: "'*Can anyone withhold water for baptizing these people, who have received the Holy Spirit just as we have?' And he commanded them to be baptized in the name of Jesus Christ*" (Acts 10:47-48). The significance of the whole of chapter 10 is that God had to do something spectacular just as he did with the Jews in Acts 2 to convince the Jewish people that Gentiles could, in fact, be Christians.

I'm thinking of being "re-baptized," does the Bible say anything about that?

While the term re-baptized is not in the Bible there are some disciples in Acts 19 who realized that their baptism was not Bible baptism, who were baptized in the Bible way. So, if you realize that you did not believe Jesus was the Son of God, or that your baptism was not for the forgiveness of sins you should follow their pattern.

I would caution you about the idea of just being baptized again because you know more now than then. If that's the case you hopefully learn more about Christianity every day and certainly to be baptized every day would be more about questioning God than becoming a Christian.

That said, if I thought my baptism was not right, I would certainly make sure rather than live in doubt.

Does it matter where I was baptized or who baptized me? I was baptized in a particular church or for a particular reason and I'm just not sure. What should I do?

Notice, this is not about location but about purpose. I never see in the Bible an emphasis on where a person was baptized or on the person baptizing them. But this is about what Jesus did and my trusting Him and obeying Him. I didn't understand all I do now about baptism when I was baptized. I didn't understand everything about the gospel and none of us did. So baptism is effective for people who don't understand everything about baptism. What other kinds of people are there?

Those from Acts 2 forward knew they knew they were sinners and they believed in Jesus. What's important is not how much the person who baptized me knew or what the name on the church building was, but did I believe in Jesus and His power to forgive sins when I followed him. Did I understand that I went into the water as a sinner and by the power of Jesus blood I came out saved. Listen closely. IF I had any question about that, I would make it sure!!! It is not worth the risk.

In 1 Corinthians 12:13a Paul reminds us that men don't decide who's in the church, God does. You are added to His body, the body of Christ when you are baptized for the forgiveness of sins (Acts 2:41). Think of it this way. Family membership is a natural consequence of birth. When my children were born, we didn't take a vote to decide if they could be in the family. They were in the family by virtue of their birth. And God put you in His family when you were born of water and of the Spirit.

What about my grandma? She wasn't baptized and she was the best most godliest person I've ever known. Are you saying she was lost?

No, it isn't my job to judge your sweet grandma, NOR is it yours. Let's let God do that. But if your grandma was as good as you say she was then she'd want you to do what you know to be right, right?

Does everybody have to be there? I'm shy and I don't want to be baptized in front of a large crowd.

No. In the Bible, there were as few as two people (the one baptizing and the one being baptized (Acts 8:36-38) and as many as thousands (Acts 2).

Am I old enough to be baptized? That's the question, isn't it?

First off, I'm really really glad you are thinking about this. I've baptized people as young as 8 and older than 80. Sometimes I wish God had just given an age but He didn't. If you think you need to be baptized then do it. We really only have the right to ask one question and that is, "Do you believe with all of your heart that Jesus is the Christ, the Son of God?"

Why Should I NOT Be Baptized?

You should not be baptized if you are doing it for the wrong reasons. Like, just because a friend was baptized, or to get out of some trouble you are in for the moment, although you don't really believe and are not really going to try to change your life. Baptism is not about getting attention. You should not be baptized if you don't understand what its purpose is or what sin is.

[1] The word brainiac is defined by *dictionary.com* as "an exceptionally intelligent person."

[2] If someone, for whatever reason, wants to try to explain baptism away, they will find a way to do it but that does not change God's Word.

COULD THERE BE MORE QUESTIONS?

1. Recap – what is baptism?

2. What is our job as Christians?

3. Do you have to know EVERYTHING before you are baptized?

4. What are some reasons not to be baptized?

5. What is the most confusing part about baptism to you?

6. Does "he who does not believe shall be condemned" (Mark 16:16b) mean that one doesn't have to be baptized to be saved? Why or why not?

7. 1 Corinthians 12:13 says that we are all baptized into one body? Whose body is it according to Ephesians 1:22-23? What is Jesus the Savior of according to Ephesians 5:23? Is it the same body one is baptized into according to 1 Corinthians 12:13?

8. Did people in the Bible who were baptized do so to please family or friends, or was it because they wanted to be saved and serve Jesus as their Lord above all for the rest of their lives?

9. Ephesians 1:22-23 says that the body of Christ, the church, is "the fullness of Him who fills all in all." In other words, the church which is the body of Christ is what fills up Christ. We are baptized into that one body (1 Corinthians 12:13). Does that have anything to do with being baptized "into Christ" (Galatians 3:27)?

10. Did Jesus give the commands to be baptized (Matthew 28:18-20; Mark 16:15-16) before or after He died and was resurrected? What covenant —the old or the new—was the command to be baptized in His name given?

LESSON 5

THAT IS ALL. IS THAT ALL?

To be clear, we love when someone makes the decision to be baptized. It is thrilling to witness or be a part of such a moment. There is not another like it anywhere. We celebrate this like nothing else. It is the one thing that camp always stops for!

At this point you might be asking: Aren't you making a bigger deal about baptism than you should?

Well, maybe. Let's talk about that.

If you think your salvation is more about water than God's power then you are making more of baptism than God did.

If you think the act of baptism is bigger than Faith then you are misunderstanding the act of baptism as an act of merit or earning and not a reaction of obeying God who has been so good to you. Remember: *"Without faith, it is impossible to please Him"* (Hebrews 11:6). So you may be dipped in water, immersed, but if it is not an action of faith then you got it wrong. I want to make a cautious observation here. My problem with applauding baptism is not that I think clapping is wrong, I don't, but that it makes the one being baptized look like he/she DID something of merit. It is God who acts in baptism, we are just servants.

If you think baptism is bigger than confession, you have over-exalted baptism. It seems possible we short change confession. It is huge biblically. *"If you do confess me before man I will confess you before the Father"* (Matthew 10:32). 2 John teaches that whoever does not confess the Son is the antiChrist (2 John 7).

If you think baptism is more an issue to be argued about than a blessing from God that puts us in His Family then you have missed the whole point! A Christian will never impact anyone if he/she is arrogant. Chill folks. We will win when we love and are true to God, not when we construct the best argument.

If you think baptism is the end, that once done, you've conquered your relationship with Jesus, then you have overblown baptism. Baptism changes your relationship with Christ, with His church, with everyone in your life. But notice it is a beginning, not an end. It is a new birth (John 3; 2 Peter 2:2).

In this lesson, I want to talk to you about "next." By their actions, it seems that some think they leave Christ in the baptistry. They don't talk His talk -- instead, their tongue belongs to the devil. They don't walk His walk, instead, they try to do what makes them happy regardless of how it makes Him feel. They said they believed He was the Son of God, but with their tongue, their time, and their talent, they act like they are their own god.

So what should I do after baptism? Let me share with you something I first heard from my dad at Maywood Christian Camp in Hamilton, Alabama at a baptism in the swimming pool there. They are the "nexts" that will make your future spiritual life RICH!

1 – Every day SAY something TO God:
This is prayer. Prayer is not a bunch of fancy words said in a church building but it is God's children talking to Him as their Father, they love, trust, respect, and want to talk to. When you are scared, hurting, angry, confused, happy, enjoying something good, depressed, tempted, unsure of what to do next, PRAY! It will

both relieve stress and will open the windows of heaven. I think this is what Paul meant when he said to *"pray without ceasing"* (1 Thessalonians 5:17).

2 – *Every day let God SAY something TO you:* If you talk to Him but don't listen to Him, those talks will not be very effective. God talks most clearly and with authority today through His Word. So, start reading His Word some every day.

Don't feel like you have to read it all in one sitting, or that you have to figure out everything about it immediately. But start. It is your spiritual food. Be hungry for it. Read some every day. For you, it may only be a few verses at first.

At first, you might just read some that you'll really enjoy -- the Gospel accounts (they're the story of Jesus life), the Psalms (they are beautiful and hopeful), some of the shorter letters to churches like Philippians (they are some of God's message to Christians). If you like to write, keep a journal nearby and make notes or write down things you don't understand. This book is the source of growing faith (Romans 10:17; 1 Peter 2:2; 2 Timothy 3:16–17).

3 – Every day SAY something FOR God: Please understand that confession is MUCH more than just a few words spoken or affirmed when you are baptized. It is the vital concept that you are not ashamed of Him, that you will talk about Him to others. Listen: When living for Christ becomes the standard in your life there will be people and that evil one who will try to break you down, but if you determine to do right and His person all the time, over time you will be respected. And, when people see you handling life by the power of His strength, and life gets tough for them, they will want to know your secrets. Jesus' last commands before going back to heaven were to tell others about Him (Matthew 28:18-20).

4 – *Every day DO something FOR God:*
The Bible says we were "created for good works" (Ephesians 2:10). Find something that you can do that is a good work and get busy doing. Start NOW. This is not something that you wait until you are older to do or wait until you have all of life figured out. You start now. If you don't know what to do, go to the leaders of the church and ask them what some things you can do are. The main thing is to start and to stick with it. If you are just doing it for attention, then find something to do that gets you no attention (Matthew 6:1). That doesn't mean no one can know about it, but it does mean to watch your motive carefully. I'd suggest finding someone else who is doing good stuff that excites you and see if you can learn from them.

5 – Every Sunday worship Him with His Family the church:

Jesus was very clear about this (Matthew 6:33) and so were His followers (Hebrews 10:25). If you determine to not follow Him or worship God then you are in sin. I know, not every sermon will be just what you believe you needed, not every song will be your favorite, not every person will overwhelm you with kindness, BUT this is not about you but about HIM. You are not there to worship you but the Lord.

6 – And, when you fall, get up:

Listen, just because you are a Christian it does not mean you will never make a mistake. Every Christian, even the best one you know, still makes them. But don't quit. You'll be glad forever that you stayed with it!

One more thing. We, the person who gave you this book, the leaders of the church, your Bible class teacher, we are all on your side. We want you to succeed spiritually. Let us know when you need help and how we can help. We are for you! And, by the way, so is the God who made heaven and earth! You can do this.

THINK IT THROUGH:

1. Can we make too big of a deal about baptism?

2. Is baptism the last step on the way to Heaven?

3. What are some "nexts" after baptism?

4. Who in your life do you trust enough that you can you talk to them about being baptized?

5. Read Matthew 6:9-15. What are some things we should pray for to God? What attitude should we have while we pray?

6. Read Psalm 1:1-3. How often should we study God's Word? What attitude should we have while we study the Bible?

7. Read Galatians 6:10. How often should we do good? Who should we do good for? What are some ways you could do good for your family, your friends, etc.? What are

some of the things YOU will do as a servant of God?

8. Read Matthew 5:16. What are some ways to let your light shine in a way to motivate the people who know you to grow closer to God and become Christians?

9. Read John 4:24. What does it mean to worship "in spirit and truth?" How can doing this make your worship at church more pleasing to God and more encouraging for you?

Thank you so much for reading this little book. I pray it has blessed your life.

If after reading it you feel the need to be baptized and need help finding someone to do it, contact me via cell, text, or email and I will get someone to you or come myself.

In God's Love,
Dale

dale@edge.net
(615) 294-1453

Other titles available from The Jenkins Institute:
The Living Word: Sermons of Jerry A. Jenkins
Before I Go: Notes from Older Preachers

Thoughts from the Mound
More Thoughts from the Mound

All I Ever Wanted to Do Was Preach
I Hope You Have to Pinch Yourself

The Preacher as Counselor
Don't Quit on a Monday
Don't Quit on a Tuesday
Don't Quit on a Wednesday
Five Secrets and a Decision
Centered: Marking Your Map in a Muddled World
On Moving Well: The Scoop-Meister's Thoughts on Ministry Transitions
Praying Always: Prayers for Preachers (gift book for ministers)

A Minister's Heart
A Youth Minister's Heart
A Mother's Heart
A Father's Heart
His Word (52 weeks of daily devotionals walking through the New Testament)

The Glory of Preaching (Jay Lockhart and Clarence DeLoach)
Profiles of Faith and Courage: Interviews with Gospel Preachers (Dennis Gulledge)
Me, You, and the People in the Pews (Tracy Moore)
From Mother's Day to Father's Day (Paul Shero)
Little Fish, Big Splash (Mark Neaves and Shawn Weaver)

Free Evangelism Resources by Jerry Jenkins:
God Speaks Today
Lovingly Leading Men to the Savior

To order, visit *thejenkinsinstitute.com/shop*